ABOUT HABITATS
Tundras

Written by **Cathryn Sill**   Illustrated by **John Sill**

PEACHTREE

ATLANTA

To the One who created tundras.
—*Genesis* 1:1

Ω

Published by
PEACHTREE PUBLISHING COMPANY INC.
1700 Chattahoochee Avenue
Atlanta, Georgia 30318-2112
PeachtreeBooks.com

Text © 2021 by Cathryn P. Sill
Illustrations © 2021 by John C. Sill

First trade paperback edition published in 2023

Edited by Vicky Holifield

Illustrations created in watercolor on archival quality 100% rag watercolor paper.

Printed and bound in July 2023 at Toppan Leefung, DongGuan, China.
10 9 8 7 6 5 4 3 2 1 (hardcover)
10 9 8 7 6 5 4 3 2 1 (trade paperback)
HC ISBN: 978-1-68263-233-8
PB ISBN: 978-1-68263-633-6

Cataloging-in-Publication Data is available from the Library of Congress.

About Habitats
Tundras

Tundras are cold, dry areas with no trees.

Most tundras are found in polar regions.

Alpine tundras are found near the tops
of very tall mountains.

PLATE 3
ALPINE TUNDRA

Siberian Ibex

Tundras have long winters. They are covered with snow much of the year.

In polar regions, the ground beneath the tundras always stays frozen.

PLATE 5
ARCTIC TUNDRA

Common Raven

Plants and animals that live in tundras have different ways of surviving cold, windy weather.

Tundra plants grow low to the ground and close together.

PLATE 7
ALPINE TUNDRA

Alpine Azalea

Many tundra plants have fuzzy stems and leaves to protect them from the cold.

PLATE 8
ARCTIC TUNDRA

Arctic Willow
Arctic Bumblebee

Most tundra animals migrate to warmer areas before winter and come back for summer.

A few animals live on the tundra through the long, harsh winter. They have warm feathers or thick fur to protect them from the cold.

PLATE 10
ARCTIC TUNDRA

Snowy Owl
Northern Collared Lemming

Some live in tunnels and dens under the snow where it is warmer.

PLATE 11
ARCTIC TUNDRA

Tundra Vole

Some hunt and eat other animals.

PLATE 12
ARCTIC TUNDRA

Arctic Wolf
Arctic Hare

Others use their feet to dig through the snow to find plants to eat.

PLATE 13
ARCTIC TUNDRA

Muskox

In the summer, warmer temperatures melt the snow on the tundra.

In summer, many birds raise their young on the tundra.

PLATE 15
ARCTIC TUNDRA

Snow Geese

They can find plenty of food and safe places to build nests during the summer.

PLATE 16
ARCTIC TUNDRA

Red Phalarope

Tundras are in danger because of pollution, rising temperatures, and harm to the land caused by too much building.

PLATE 17
ARCTIC TUNDRA

Tundras are important places that need to be protected.

Tundras

Afterword

PLATE 1

The tundra biome covers about one fifth of Earth's land surface. The name tundra comes from *tuntaria*, a Finnish word that means "treeless plain." Trees and other large plants are unable to grow in tundras because of low temperatures, short growing seasons, and poor soil. Arctic Foxes are one of the few animals that stay in Arctic tundras year-round. They live in parts of North America, northern Europe, and northern Asia.

PLATE 2

The Arctic and Antarctic tundras are found between the frozen polar ice caps and the warmer land where trees can grow. The largest areas of tundra are in the Arctic. Antarctica has less tundra habitat because most of the continent is covered in ice. It cannot support many plants and land animals. During the warmer season, some marine animals such as seals and Gentoo Penguins move to the Subantarctic tundra to raise their young. South Polar Skuas are seabirds that hunt and eat other animals, including young penguins.

PLATE 3

Alpine tundras are found above the tree line on tall mountains all around much of the world. The weather in alpine tundras is cold and windy. Ibex and some other alpine tundra animals migrate up and down the mountains as the seasons change. During warmer seasons, Siberian Ibex find grasses and herbs to eat in tundra and alpine meadows. They live on mountains in central Asia and southern Siberia.

PLATE 4

In the Arctic and Antarctic the sun never rises in midwinter. Any snow that falls on the tundras stays there all winter. Alpine tundras have longer days but are still so cold the snow does not melt until summer. Ptarmigans, birds in the grouse family, can survive the long winters in both arctic and alpine tundras. Most of them turn white in winter. In summer, their feathers are brown. Willow Ptarmigans live in Arctic tundras.

PLATE 5

Underneath the surface of polar tundras is a layer of ground called "permafrost," which stays frozen permanently. It is impossible for plants to grow deep roots in the permafrost. The hard frozen ground causes the roots to grow sideways instead of down. Alpine tundras do not have permafrost unless they are close to polar regions or on extremely high mountains. Common Ravens live in tundras and in many other habitats across the Northern Hemisphere.

PLATE 6

Tundras have frigid winter weather with temperatures sometimes as low as -58° Fahrenheit (-50° Celsius). Winds may blow at speeds of 30 to 60 miles per hour (48 to 97 kilometers per hour). Most plants and animals are not able to survive such harsh conditions. Purple Saxifrage is a hardy plant that lives in Arctic and alpine tundras. It begins to bloom as soon as the snow starts melting. Its edible flowers are a common food for Arctic Hares. Arctic Hares live in the northern parts of North America, including Greenland.

PLATE 7

Several types of mosses, grasses, sedges, short shrubs, and other flowering plants live in tundras. Because these plants grow low and close together, they are protected from the wind and less heat escapes from the soil around them. Some plants are able to grow under the snow. Lichens are also common in tundras. Alpine Azaleas are short shrubs that grow in both Arctic and alpine tundras in the Northern Hemisphere.

PLATE 8

The small hairs on many tundra plants trap warm air and give protection from the wind. Some tundra insects such as Arctic Bumblebees also have thick hair on their bodies. Arctic Bumblebees hibernate in winter. In summer they pollinate many flowers, including Arctic Willows. Arctic Bumblebees and Arctic Willows are both circumpolar in the Northern Hemisphere.

PLATE 9

Before winter sets in, some Arctic tundra animals migrate to nearby forests where they are more protected from the cold. Many birds migrate long distances away from the tundra. Alpine migrants may move down the mountains to find food and warmer places. Caribou migrations are the longest of any land animal. Large herds of Caribou often travel together along the same routes. Caribou are circumpolar in the Arctic tundras and surrounding forests.

PLATE 10

Animals that live in tundras year-round store up fat to help them get through the winter. Some birds have feathers on their feet to protect them from the cold. Some mammals such as Northern Collared Lemmings have fur on the soles of their feet. They are gray in summer and white in winter. Northern Collared Lemmings live in North America, including Greenland. Snowy Owls are circumpolar in the Northern Hemisphere.

PLATE 11

A few animals in tundras hibernate, but most of them deal with the cold in other ways. Many stay active under the snow all winter. The snow acts like a warm blanket that helps protect them from strong winds and cold temperatures. Tundra Voles tunnel through the snow in winter. They store seeds and roots in underground burrows to eat. Tundra Voles live in parts of North America, including Greenland; Europe; and Asia.

PLATE 12

In the snowy winter, the fur of many tundra animals is white. White fur acts as camouflage that helps predators sneak up on prey. Prey may also have white fur to help them hide. Some of these animals turn brown in summer. Arctic Wolves stay white all year. One of their main prey is Arctic Hares. Arctic Wolves live in the Canadian Arctic and Greenland.

PLATE 13

In summer, herbivores eat flowers, seeds, berries, grass, and shrubs. In winter, they eat plants they find underneath the snow. Muskoxen are large herbivores that use their hooves and noses to dig through the snow to look for roots, mosses, lichens, and the bark from shrubs. They are native to parts of North America including Greenland but have been introduced to other parts of the Arctic.

PLATE 14

Summers are longer in alpine tundras than in the Arctic and Antarctic. Even with warmer weather, the temperature usually falls below freezing at night. Food—grasses, leaves, flowers, fruits, seeds, and roots—is plentiful during alpine summers. American Pikas gather grasses and flowers and pile them in the sun to dry out. They store the dried plants under rocks for winter food. American Pikas live on rocky slopes in western North America.

PLATE 15

Millions of shorebirds, songbirds, swans, ducks, and geese migrate to tundras each summer to build nests, lay eggs, and raise chicks. Days are long and food is plentiful. Young birds grow up quickly in this habitat because the summers are so short. Baby Snow Geese can walk and leave the nest within a few hours after hatching. They are able to fly in 42 to 50 days. Snow Geese nest in North America, Greenland, and the northeastern tip of Siberia.

PLATE 16

Clouds of mosquitoes, blackflies, gnats, and other insects hatch in pools created by melting snow. The swarms of insects provide food for many birds that nest in the tundra. Red Phalarope chicks leave the nest as soon as they hatch. Unlike most other birds, the male Red Phalarope has duller colors than the female and raises the young by himself. After the female lays eggs, she starts migrating to the ocean. Red Phalaropes spend winter on the open ocean and the summer in the Arctic tundra in North America and Eurasia.

PLATE 17

Tundras are easily damaged. People mine them for valuable resources including oil, natural gas, diamonds, and other minerals. Road construction, mining, and drilling operations interrupt animal migrations, increase the danger of oil spills, and cause other forms of pollution. Climate change is one of the main threats to tundras. Warming temperatures are melting the permafrost, causing changes that endanger the plants and animals that live there.

PLATE 18

Because of the short growing season, it takes a long time for tundras to recover if they are harmed. Tundras are home to an amazing group of plants and animals. They provide an opportunity for people to see and study these unique forms of life. Protecting tundras from damage caused by development, air pollution, and climate change calls for careful consideration. Tundra Swans migrate many miles in order to nest on the Arctic Tundra. Like all animals, they need clean, safe places to raise their young. Tundra Swans live in North America.

GLOSSARY

BIOME—an area such as a forest or a wetland that shares the same types of plants and animals
ECOSYSTEM—a community of living things and their environment
HABITAT—the place where animals and plants live

circumpolar—referring to the area found around one of Earth's poles
continent—one of seven large areas of land on Earth
herbivore—an animal that eats plants
lichen—a plantlike organism that is a combination of fungus and alga
moss—a small flowerless green plant that grows in damp areas
Northern Hemisphere—the northern half of Earth
predator—an animal that lives by hunting and eating other animals
prey—an animal that is hunted and eaten by a predator
sedge—a grasslike plant that usually grows in wet ground
shrub—a low woody plant smaller than a tree; a bush
tree line—the place in a habitat where trees can no longer grow because of harsh conditions

BIBLIOGRAPHY

Books

Tundras by Erinn Banting (AV2 by Weigl)
Life in a Tundra by Kari Schuetz (Bellwether Media)
Tundra Biomes by Louise A. Spilsbury and Richard Spilsbury (Crabtree Publishing Company)
Tundra Biomes around the World by Phillip Simpson (Capstone Press)

Websites

"Arctic Tundra," www.kidzone.ws/habitats/arctic-tundra.htm
"Tundra," www.dkfindout.com/us/animals-and-nature/habitats-and-ecosystems/tundra
"Kids Do Ecology: World Biomes," kids.nceas.ucsb.edu/biomes/tundra.html
"ThoughtCo.: Tundra Biome," www.thoughtco.com/tundra-biome-130801
"Wildlife Journal Junior: Tundra," www.nhpbs.org/wild/tundra.asp

ABOUT... SERIES

HC: 978-1-68263-031-0
PB: 978-1-68263-032-7

HC: 978-1-56145-038-1
PB: 978-1-56145-364-1

HC: 978-1-56145-688-8
PB: 978-1-56145-699-4

HC: 978-1-56145-301-6
PB: 978-1-56145-405-1

HC: 978-1-56145-987-2
PB: 978-1-56145-988-9

HC: 978-1-56145-588-1
PB: 978-1-56145-837-0

PB: 978-1-56145-882-0

HC: 978-1-56145-757-1
PB: 978-1-56145-758-8

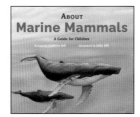

HC: 978-1-56145-906-3
PB: 978-1-68263-288-8

HC: 978-1-56145-358-0
PB: 978-1-56145-407-5

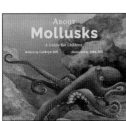

PB: 978-1-56145-406-8

HC: 978-1-56145-795-3
PB: 978-1-68263-158-4

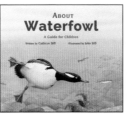

PB: 978-1-56145-741-0

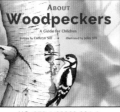

HC: 978-1-56145-536-2
PB: 978-1-56145-811-0

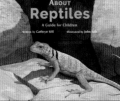

HC: 978-1-56145-907-0
PB: 978-1-56145-908-7

PB: 978-1-56145-914-8

HC: 978-1-68263-092-1

HC: 978-1-68263-234-5

HC: 978-1-68263-004-4

ALSO AVAILABLE IN SPANISH AND ENGLISH/SPANISH EDITIONS

• About Amphibians / Sobre los anfibios PB: 978-1-68263-033-4 • Sobre los anfibios PB: 978-1-68263-230-7 • About Birds / Sobre los pájaros PB: 978-1-56145-783-0
• Sobre los pájaros PB: 978-1-68263-071-6 • About Fish / Sobre los peces PB: 978-1-56145-989-6 • Sobre los peces PB: 978-1-68263-154-6
• About Insects / Sobre los insectos PB: 978-1-56145-883-7 • Sobre los insectos PB: 978-1-68263-155-3 • About Mammals / Sobre los mamíferos PB: 978-1-56145-800-4
• Sobre los mamíferos PB: 978-1-68263-072-3 • About Reptiles / Sobre los reptiles PB: 978-1-56145-909-4 • Sobre los reptiles PB: 978-1-68263-231-4

ABOUT HABITATS SERIES

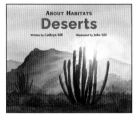

ABOUT HABITATS
Deserts
Written by Cathryn Sill   Illustrated by John Sill

PB: 978-1-56145-636-9

ABOUT HABITATS
Forests
Written by Cathryn Sill   Illustrated by John Sill

HC: 978-1-56145-734-2
PB: 978-1-68263-126-3

ABOUT HABITATS
Grasslands
Written by Cathryn Sill   Illustrated by John Sill

HC: 978-1-56145-559-1
PB: 978-1-68263-034-1

ABOUT HABITATS
Mountains
Written by Cathryn Sill   Illustrated by John Sill

HC: 978-1-56145-469-3
PB: 978-1-56145-731-1

ABOUT HABITATS
Oceans
Written by Cathryn Sill   Illustrated by John Sill

HC: 978-1-56145-618-5
PB: 978-1-56145-960-5

ABOUT HABITATS
Polar Regions
Written by Cathryn Sill   Illustrated by John Sill

HC: 978-1-56145-832-5
PB: 978-1-68263-334-2

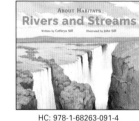

ABOUT HABITATS
Rivers and Streams
Written by Cathryn Sill   Illustrated by John Sill

HC: 978-1-68263-091-4
PB: 978-1-68263-394-6

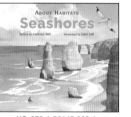

ABOUT HABITATS
Seashores
Written by Cathryn Sill   Illustrated by John Sill

HC: 978-1-56145-968-1
PB: 978-1-68263-402-8

ABOUT HABITATS
Tundras
Written by Cathryn Sill   Illustrated by John Sill

HC: 978-1-68263-233-8
PB: 978-1-68263-633-6

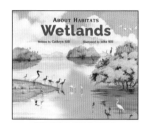

ABOUT HABITATS
Wetlands
Written by Cathryn Sill   Illustrated by John Sill

PB: 978-1-56145-689-5

THE SILLS

CATHRYN AND JOHN SILL are the talented team who created the *About…* series as well as the *About Habitats* series. Their books have garnered praise from educators and have won a variety of awards, including Bank Street Best Books, CCBC Choices, NSTA/CBC Outstanding Science Trade Books for Students K–12, Orbis Pictus Recommended, and *Science Books & Films* Best Books of the Year. Cathryn, a graduate of Western Carolina University, taught early elementary school classes for thirty years. John holds a BS in wildlife biology from North Carolina State University. Combining his artistic skill and knowledge of wildlife, he has achieved an impressive reputation as a wildlife artist. The Sills live in Franklin, North Carolina.

Fred Eldredge, Creative Image Photography